BIG PICTURE 📷 SPORTS

Meet the
CAROLINA
PANTHERS

By
ZACK BURGESS

NORWOOD HOUSE 🏠 PRESS

CHICAGO, ILLINOIS

NORWOOD HOUSE 🏠 PRESS

P.O. Box 316598 • Chicago, Illinois 60631
For more information about Norwood House Press please visit our website at
www.norwoodhousepress.com or call 866-565-2900.

Photo Credits:
All photos courtesy of Associated Press, except for the following: Black Book Archives (6, 15, 18, 22, 23),
Topps, Inc. (10 top, 11 middle), Pacific Trading Cards (10 bottom), Fleer Corp. (11 top),
Panini America (11 bottom).

Cover Photo: Bob Leverone/Associated Press

The football memorabilia photographed for this book is part of the authors' collection. The collectibles used
for artistic background purposes in this series were manufactured by many different card companies—
including Bowman, Donruss, Fleer, Leaf, O-Pee-Chee, Pacific, Panini America, Philadelphia Chewing Gum,
Pinnacle, Pro Line, Pro Set, Score, Topps, and Upper Deck—as well as several food brands, including
Crane's, Hostess, Kellogg's, McDonald's and Post.

Designer: Ron Jaffe
Series Editors: Mike Kennedy and Mark Stewart
Project Management: Black Book Partners, LLC.
Editorial Production: Lisa Walsh

LIBRARY OF CONGRESS CATALOGING-IN-PUBLICATION DATA
Names: Burgess, Zack.
Title: Meet the Carolina Panthers / by Zack Burgess.
Description: Chicago, Illinois : Norwood House Press, 2016. | Series: Big
    picture sports | Includes bibliographical references and index.
Identifiers: LCCN 2015026315| ISBN 9781599537412 (library edition : alk.
    paper) | ISBN 9781603578448 (ebook)
Subjects: LCSH: Carolina Panthers (Football team)--History--Juvenile
    literature.
Classification: LCC GV956.C27 B87 2016 | DDC 796.332/640975676--dc23
LC record available at http://lccn.loc.gov/2015026315

288N—072016
Manufactured in the United States of America in North Mankato, Minnesota

CONTENTS

Words in **bold type** are defined on page 24.

The Panthers celebrate a scoring play.

CALL ME A PANTHER

People in North Carolina and South Carolina love football. The Carolina Panthers know this better than anyone. The Panthers play with speed and smarts. They pounce on mistakes by opponents. How else would you expect a panther to play?

TIME MACHINE

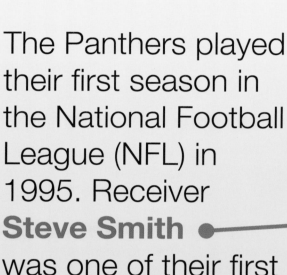

The Panthers played their first season in the National Football League (NFL) in 1995. Receiver **Steve Smith** ● ⟶ was one of their first big stars. In 2011, Cam Newton joined the Panthers. He led them to the Super Bowl in 2016.

Cam Newton lets the fans know he hears them.

Fans enjoy a Panthers game on a sunny day.

Best Seat in the House

The Panthers play in Charlotte, North Carolina. The city is close to the South Carolina border. The team's stadium was built in 1996. In 2014, it was updated to make games even more fun for fans.

SHOE BOX

The trading cards on these pages show some of the best Panthers ever.

SAM MILLS

LINEBACKER · 1995-1997

Sam was a fearless tackling machine. Fans called him the "Field Mouse" for his speed, quickness, and leadership.

WESLEY WALLS

TIGHT END · 1996-2002

Wesley was a talented receiver and blocker. He played in the **Pro Bowl** five times as a Panther.

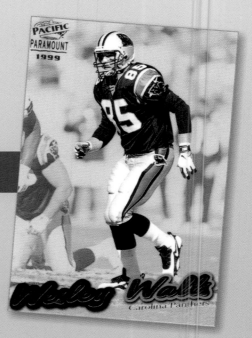

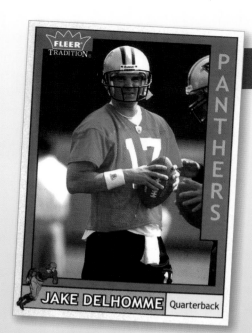

JAKE DELHOMME

QUARTERBACK · 2003-2009

Jake began 2003 as the team's backup quarterback. He became the starter and led the Panthers to their first Super Bowl.

JAKE DELHOMME | Quarterback

JULIUS PEPPERS

DEFENSIVE END · 2002-2009

Julius was quick and powerful. He had 81 **quarterback sacks** for the Panthers.

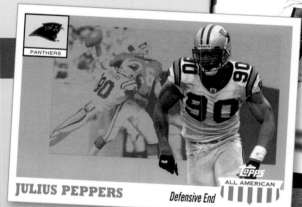

JULIUS PEPPERS | Defensive End

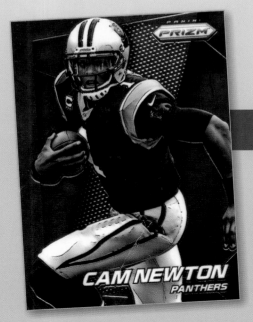

CAM NEWTON | PANTHERS

CAM NEWTON

QUARTERBACK · FIRST YEAR WITH TEAM: 2011

Cam could beat opponents with his arm or his legs. He combined for 45 passing and rushing touchdowns in 2015.

11

THE BIG PICTURE

Look at the two photos on page 13. Both appear to be the same. But they are not. There are three differences. Can you spot them?

Answers on page 23.

TRUE OR FALSE?

Steve Smith was a star receiver. Two of these facts about him are **TRUE**. One is **FALSE**. Do you know which is which?

1. Steve caught 103 passes for the Panthers in 2005.

2. As a boy, Steve dressed as a panther every Halloween.

3. Steve scored the Panthers' first-ever Super Bowl touchdown.

14

Answer on page 23.

Steve Smith makes a one-handed catch.

Kids have a great time at Panthers games.

Go Panthers, Go!

Panthers fans make a lot of noise at home games. Some of the team's most loyal fans are children. Sometimes they scream louder than the adults sitting around them. They love to celebrate with players after a Carolina touchdown.

ON THE MAP

Here is a look at where five Panthers were born, along with a fun fact about each.

1 **JORDAN GROSS · NAMPA, IDAHO**
Jordan was the star of Carolina's offensive line for 11 seasons.

2 **RYAN KALIL · TUCSON, ARIZONA**
Ryan was one of the quickest centers in NFL history.

3 **LUKE KUECHLY · CINCINNATI, OHIO**
Luke was an **All-Pro** in three of his first four seasons.

4 **KERRY COLLINS · LEBANON, PENNSYLVANIA**
Kerry was the team's first-ever **draft pick**.

5 **STAR LOTULELEI · TONGA**
Star anchored the defensive line for the Panthers' 2016 Super Bowl team.

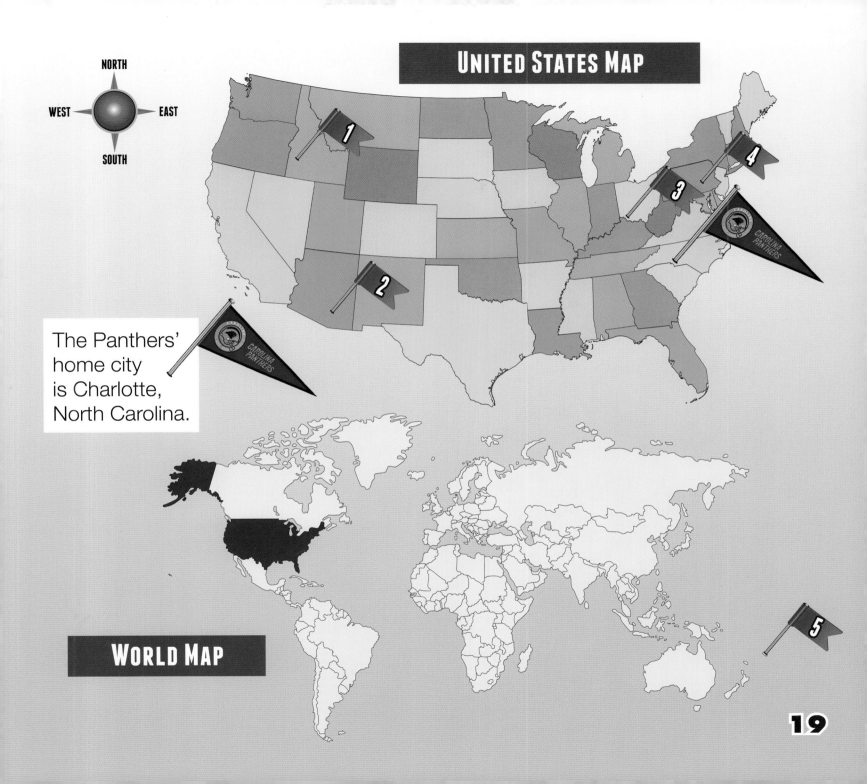

UNITED STATES MAP

NORTH
WEST — EAST
SOUTH

The Panthers'
home city
is Charlotte,
North Carolina.

WORLD MAP

19

Luke Kuechly wears the Panthers' home uniform.

Football teams wear different uniforms for home and away games. Carolina's colors are light blue, silver, black, and white. The team sometimes wears white jerseys at home to stay cool.

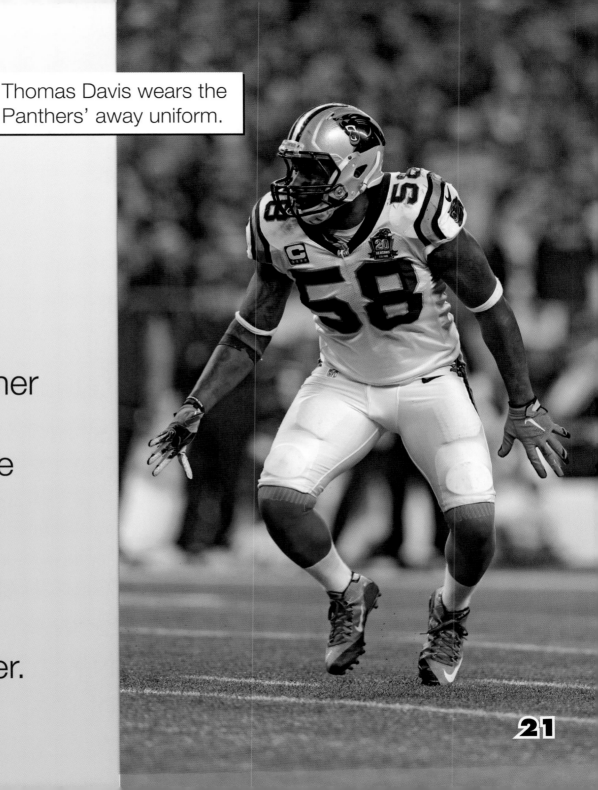

Thomas Davis wears the Panthers' away uniform.

The Panthers' helmet is silver. It shows a panther on each side. The shape of the panther looks a little like the outline of North and South Carolina together.

The Panthers reached their first Super Bowl in 2004. That season, coach **John Fox** led a team that beat opponents with great defense. The Panthers returned to the Super Bowl in 2016. Cam Newton was the star of that team.

RECORD BOOK

These Panthers set team records.

TOUCHDOWN PASSES		RECORD
Season:	Steve Beuerlein (1999)	36
Career:	Jake Delhomme	120

TOUCHDOWN CATCHES		RECORD
Season:	**Muhsin Muhammad** (2004)	16
Career:	Steve Smith	67

RUSHING TOUCHDOWNS		RECORD
Season:	DeAngelo Williams (2008)	18
Career:	DeAngelo Williams	46

ANSWERS FOR THE BIG PICTURE
The 8 in #28 changed to 0, the stripes on #1's helmet changed color, and the C on #1's jersey disappeared.

ANSWER FOR TRUE AND FALSE
#2 is false. Steve never dressed as a panther as a kid.

FOOTBALL WORDS

INDEX

All-Pro
An honor given to the best NFL player at each position.

Draft Pick
A player selected during the NFL's meeting each spring.

Pro Bowl
The NFL's annual all-star game.

Quarterback Sacks
Tackles of the quarterback that lose yardage.

Photos are on **BOLD** numbered pages.

ABOUT THE AUTHOR

Zack Burgess has been writing about sports for more than 20 years. He has lived all over the country and interviewed lots of All-Pro football players, including Brett Favre, Eddie George, Jerome Bettis, Shannon Sharpe, and Rich Gannon. Zack was the first African American beat writer to cover Major League Baseball when he worked for the *Kansas City Star*.

ABOUT THE PANTHERS

Learn more at these websites:

www.panthers.com • www.profootballhof.com

www.teamspiritextras.com/Overtime/html/panthers.html